TIME for KIDS
AMAZING ATHLETES

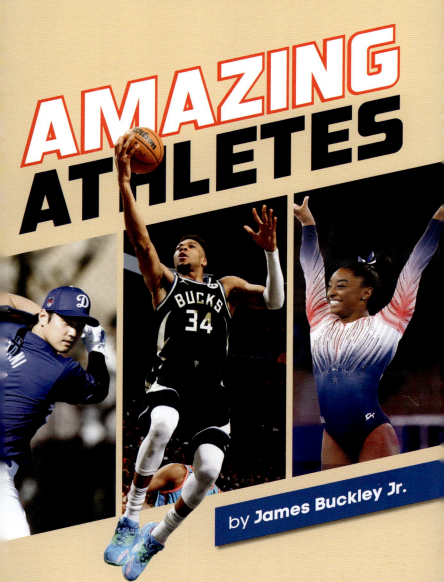

by James Buckley Jr.

PENGUIN YOUNG READERS LICENSES
An imprint of Penguin Random House LLC, New York

First published in the United States of America by Penguin Young Readers Licenses,
an imprint of Penguin Random House LLC, New York, 2024

TIME for Kids © 2024 TIME USA, LLC. All Rights Reserved.

Penguin supports copyright. Copyright fuels creativity, encourages diverse voices,
promotes free speech, and creates a vibrant culture. Thank you for buying an authorized
edition of this book and for complying with copyright laws by not reproducing, scanning,
or distributing any part of it in any form without permission. You are supporting writers
and allowing Penguin to continue to publish books for every reader.

Visit us online at penguinrandomhouse.com

Library of Congress Cataloging-in-Publication Data is available.

Manufactured in China

ISBN 9780593754948   10 9 8 7 6 5 4 3 2 1 TOPL

Design by Hsiao-Pin Lin and Abby Dening

The publisher does not have any control over and does not assume any responsibility
for author or third-party websites or their content.

• • • • • • • • • • • • • •

Photo credits: Cover: Alamy: (Simone Biles) Richard Ellis/UPI, (Travis Kelce) Trask Smith/ZUMA Wire. **Getty Images:** (football) kledge/E+, (Giannis Antetokounmpo) Barry Gossage/NBAE, (lights) chiewr/iStock, (Shohei Ohtani) Chris Coduto/Getty Images Sport, (soccer ball) ilbusca/E+, (tennis ball) stockcam/E+, (tennis racket) C-You/iStock. **Interior: Alamy:** 1: (Simone Biles) Richard Ellis/UPI; 6: (top) Thurman James/Cal Sport Media, (bottom) Frank Molter/Alamy Live News; 7: (top) Laurence Kesterson/UPI, (bottom) Michael Sullivan/Cal Sport Media; 8: (top) Brandon Sloter/Image of Sport, (bottom) Aaron Josefczyk/UPI; 9: Jon Endow/Image of Sport; 10–11: Paul Kitagaki Jr./ZUMA Press Wire; 12: (top) Felipe Mondino/Independent Photo Agency, (bottom) Martin Rickett; 13: JP Waldron/Cal Sport Media; 14: Stephen Nadler/PX Imagens/ZUMA Press Wire; 15: (bottom) PCN Photography; 16: Steve Faber/Cal Sport Media; 17: Bill Greenblatt/UPI; 18: Irina R Hipolito/DPPI/LiveMedia/Independent Photo Agency; 19: Meng Dingbo/Xinhua; 20–21: Marty Jean-Louis; 22–23: Chris Putnam; 24: GONZALEZ OSCAR; 25: (top) Chris Putnam/ZUMA Press Wire, (bottom) Gian Mattia D'Alberto/LaPresse; 26: (top) Shaina Benhiyoun/SPP Sport Press Photo, (bottom) Paolo Pizzi/Pacific Press/Sipa USA; 27: Marty Jean-Louis; 28: (top) Yohei Osada/AFLO SPORT, (bottom) Stephen A. Arce/ASP/ZUMA Wire; 29: (top) Colleen Claggett/SPP Sport Press Photo, (bottom) James Atoa/UPI; 30: Erik Kabik Photography/Media Punch; 31: Lev Radin/Pacific Press/ZUMA Press Wire; 32: Kim Hukari/Image of Sport; 33: Erik Flaaris Johansen/NTB; 34: Belga News Agency; 35: Ringo Chiu/SOPA Images/Sipa USA; 36: (top) John Fisher/Cal Sport Media, (bottom) Archie Carpenter/UPI; 37: (top) Kim Price/Cal Sport Media, (bottom) Eric Canha/Cal Sport Media; 38: Naoki Morita/AFLO SPORT; 39: Thurman James/Cal Sport Media; 40: David Tulis/UPI; 41: Reggie Hildred/Cal Sport Media; 42–43: Ringo Chiu/ZUMA Press Wire; 44: Marty Jean-Louis; 45: Chris Poss; 46–47: John Angelillo/UPI; 48: (top) Jon Robichaud/UPI, (bottom) Peter Dovgan/UK Sports Pics Ltd; 49: Ding Ting/Xinhua; 50: Paul Sutton-PCN; 51: (top) Jj Jung/ZUMA Press Wire, (bottom) Philippe Millereau/KMSP/DPPI; 52: Elyanna Garcia/SPP Sport Press Photo; 53: Shaun Brooks/Action Plus Sports; 54–55: Bernd Thissen/dpa; 56: Kyle Okita/Cal Sport Media; 57: Ulrik Pedersen/NurPhoto; 58: Martin Rickett/PA Images; 59: (top) Dominique Mollee/ANP, (bottom) IOS/Espa-Images; 60: Dan Anderson/ZUMA Press Wire; 61: Nicholas T. LoVerde/Cal Sport Media; 62: (top) Henrik Montgomery/TT News Agency, (bottom) Jean Catuffe/DPPI; 63: Spencer Lee/ZUMA Press Wire; 64: (top) John Walton/PA Images, (bottom) Zac Goodwin/PA Images; 65: (top) Wang Ying/Xinhua, (bottom) David Woodley/Action Plus Sports; 66–67: Greg Atkins/Cal Sport Media; 68: MATSUO.K/AFLO SPORT; 69: IMAGO/Erik Kabik Photography/Media Punch; 70: Richard Nicholson/UK Sports Pics Ltd; 71: Laurent Lairys/Abaca Press; 72: Peter Schatz; 73: Rich Barnes/Cal Sport Media; 74: Mark Edward Harris/ZUMA Press Wire; 75: Katy Blackwood; 76: Cory Royster/Cal Sport Media; 77: (top) Grace Schultz/Cal Sport Media, (bottom) Shaina Benhiyoun/SPP Sport Press Photo; 78–79: Victor Fraile/Power Sport Images; 80: Independent Photo Agency; 81: (top) Anthony Behar/Sipa USA, (bottom) Zac Goodwin/PA Images; 82–83: Michael Kappeler/dpa; 84: (top) Ryan Asman, (bottom) Pete Dovgan/Speed Media; 85: (top) Brandon Sloter/Image of Sport, (bottom) Larry Marano/UPI; 86–87: Shaina Benhiyoun/SPP Sport Press Photo; 88: (top) Joel Lerner/Xinhua, (bottom) Erica Denhoff/Cal Sport Media; 89: Jonathan Tenca/Cal Sport Media; 90–91: Peter Joneleit/Cal Sport Media; 92: (top) Tom Walko/Image of Sport, (bottom) Tim Goode/PA Images; 93: John Walton/PA Images; 94: Javier Vicencio/Eyepix Group. **Bart Boatwright:** 15: (top). **Getty Images:** 1: (Giannis Antetokounmpo) Barry Gossage/NBAE, (Shohei Ohtani) Chris Coduto/Getty Images Sport; 2–3: filo/E+; 4–5: (glove) ronniechua/iStock, (lacrosse stick) cmannphoto/iStock; 95: (ball, glove, helmet) herreid/iStock.

CONTENTS

- 04 Introduction
- 06 A
- 09 B
- 15 C
- 22 D
- 28 E
- 30 F
- 31 G
- 33 H
- 39 I
- 40 J
- 48 K
- 52 L
- 59 M
- 72 N
- 74 O
- 76 P
- 78 R
- 81 S
- 86 T
- 92 V
- 94 W
- 95 Resources
- 96 Index

INTRODUCTION

They run, jump, throw, dive, swim, drive, skate, bat, tackle—and score way, way better than the average person. They're the athletes who play our favorite sports and who bring us thrills, joy, and sometimes, disappointment. But that's sports. You win some, you lose some. In this book, we celebrate the very best of a wide variety of sports. We hope your favorites are in here—but we also hope you'll discover some new favorites! Maybe you'll even discover a sport to watch or play. The stats and bios in this book were updated through February 2024, so there are plenty of athletes you might have recently watched featured right here.

We chose athletes who were active when we wrote the book, so you won't see stars who've recently retired. We tried to find athletes who are making news and breaking barriers: Their journeys are ever-changing. Start with their stories here, then use TIME for Kids and other trusted media to follow their amazing careers.

All of these athletes are champions, but they didn't start out that way. They began their journey to success long ago when they were kids. They learned their game, studied the rules, got in shape, and then it was practice, practice, practice. No one becomes a superstar athlete overnight. It takes years of dedication and energy. As you read these stories of top sports stars, think about how you might start to make your own dreams come true—on the field, the diamond, the court, the rink, the track, or wherever else you choose!

SPORTS CHECKLIST

Make sure you cover the wide, wide world of sports. Check off each sport you find as you read about the athletes, who are featured in alphabetical order.

- ☐ Auto Racing
- ☐ Baseball
- ☐ Basketball
- ☐ Figure Skating
- ☐ Football
- ☐ Golf
- ☐ Gymnastics
- ☐ Ice Hockey
- ☐ Lacrosse
- ☐ Skateboarding
- ☐ Skiing
- ☐ Snowboarding
- ☐ Soccer
- ☐ Softball
- ☐ Surfing
- ☐ Swimming
- ☐ Tennis
- ☐ Track and Field

RONALD ACUÑA JR.

Baseball

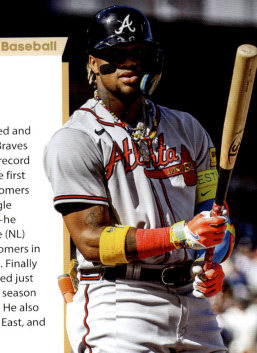

With a rare mix of speed and power, this Atlanta Braves star is rewriting the record books. In 2023, he became the first player ever with 40 or more homers and 70 or more steals in a single season. After a brilliant start—he was the 2018 National League (NL) Rookie of the Year—and 41 homers in 2019, **ACUÑA** battled injuries. Finally fully healthy, in 2023 he showed just what he could do, ending the season with 41 homers and 73 steals. He also helped the Braves win the NL East, and was then named the NL MVP.

CARLOS ALCARAZ

Tennis

Men's tennis has been dominated by three stars for almost two decades: Roger Federer, Rafael Nadal, and Novak Djokovic. In 2023, a young Spanish star seemed like a good bet to break into the top ranks. After winning the 2022 US Open, **ALCARAZ** beat Djokovic to win Wimbledon in 2023. He has already won more than 150 matches and been ranked No. 1 in the world before he turned twenty-one.

JOSH ALLEN — Football

The University of Wyoming has not sent many players to the National Football League (NFL), but one Cowboy has certainly made a big mark. Josh **ALLEN** was the Buffalo Bills' first draft pick in 2018, and he was the starter soon after. He has had three seasons with 30 or more touchdown passes and has led the Bills to the playoffs four times. Allen is also a tough runner, able to use his strength and size to score on the ground.

JOCELYN ALO — Softball

No one has had more success as a college softball hitter than **ALO**. She finished her four years at the University of Oklahoma as the National Collegiate Athletic Association (NCAA) all-time leader in homers, slugging percentage, and total bases. She had a record 12 homers in College World Series play, helping her team win back-to-back titles in 2021 and 2022. She was the player of the year twice, as well as the 2022 ESPY Award's Best College Athlete in women's sports.

PETE ALONSO
Baseball

You have to love his nickname: Polar Bear. **ALONSO** has been putting the freeze on big-league pitchers since he burst onto the scene as a member of the New York Mets with a rookie-record 53 homers in 2019. He's been slugging ever since, with two more 40-homer seasons and a league-best 131 RBIs (runs batted in) in 2022. Alonso might strike out often, but when he connects—it's magic!

GIANNIS ANTETOKOUNMPO
Basketball

It's a long way from the streets of Athens, Greece, to the top of the National Basketball Association (NBA), but **ANTETOKOUNMPO** has made it. As a kid in Greece, the future two-time NBA MVP had to sell CDs and watches in the street to help his family. He discovered basketball at a sports club and soon became a star. The Milwaukee Bucks chose him in the first round of the 2013 draft when he was only eighteen. His all-around excellence has helped the Bucks reach the playoffs eight times, including an NBA title in 2021. He's nearly seven feet tall but can move like a guard, and he's also one of the league's top defenders.

MOOKIE BETTS — Baseball

Win a trivia contest by knowing that this all-around superstar's real first name is actually Markus! Whatever you call him, he's a winner. Originally an infielder, **BETTS** joined the Boston Red Sox in 2014. He was an All-Star by 2016 and the American League (AL) MVP in 2018, as he led the AL in batting average and led Boston to a World Series win. Incredibly, the Sox traded Betts to the LA Dodgers . . . and he led *them* to a World Series title, too (in 2020).

SIMONE BILES

Gymnastics

In the high-flying, gravity-defying sport of gymnastics, there is only one GOAT. And we don't mean the furry kind. **BILES** is the "Greatest of All Time" at one of history's oldest sports. Through 2023, she has an incredible twenty-three world championship gold medals (and thirty medals overall), by far the most of all time. In 2016, she dominated the Olympics, winning four golds. She even has five gymnastics moves named after her! Biles was adopted by her grandparents; she was a bouncy, active kid growing up in Texas. She discovered gymnastics when she was six and never looked back. After becoming a junior champion, Biles won her first US national title in 2013. A few months later, she was the world all-around champ, a title she earned five more times! That led to her triumph at the Games in Rio de Janeiro in 2016. Biles thrilled fans around the world with her powerful leaps on the vault, her soaring spins in the floor exercises, and her daring on the balance beam. In 2021, during the Tokyo Olympics, Biles received praise for speaking out about her mental health after she dropped out of some events. She taught many people about the need to understand the role mental health plays in all our lives. At the 2023 World Championships, she won the all-around for the sixth time, led the US team to its seventh straight gold, and added three individual golds. Biles is only four feet, eight inches tall, but she's a giant in the world of sports.

AITANA BONMATÍ

Soccer

Bonmatí saw her soccer dreams come true in 2023 when she led Spain to its first Women's World Cup championship. The creative and hardworking midfielder was named the winner of the FIFA Golden Ball as the tournament's top player, to go with her trophy as the top player in European soccer. In 2023, **BONMATÍ** won her first Ballon d'Or trophy as the best player in the world! She stars with FC Barcelona when she's not wearing Spain's colors.

DEVIN BOOKER

Basketball

Booker has been pouring in points since he joined the Phoenix Suns in 2015 at the age of eighteen. When he scored his 1,000th career point in 2016, he was the fourth youngest player ever to reach that mark. **BOOKER** has really blossomed in recent seasons. He led the Suns to the NBA Finals in 2021 and to a team record of 64 wins in 2021–22. Booker also earned an Olympic gold medal with Team USA in 2021.

JOE BURROW

Football

In 2023, **BURROW** signed what was then the biggest contract in NFL history: five years for $275 million! He had given the Cincinnati Bengals new life. Burrow had led LSU to the national college title in 2019 and was the Bengals' number-one overall pick in 2020. After recovering from a knee injury, in 2021 he led the Bengals to the Super Bowl (they lost to the Los Angeles Rams), and he was the "Comeback Player of the Year." *Ka-ching!*

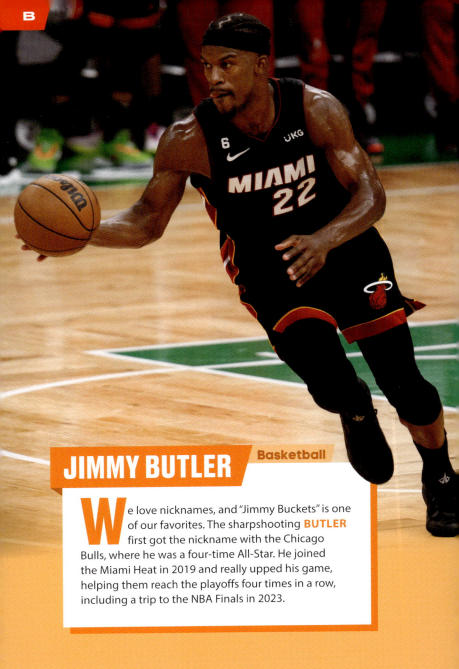

JIMMY BUTLER — Basketball

We love nicknames, and "Jimmy Buckets" is one of our favorites. The sharpshooting **BUTLER** first got the nickname with the Chicago Bulls, where he was a four-time All-Star. He joined the Miami Heat in 2019 and really upped his game, helping them reach the playoffs four times in a row, including a trip to the NBA Finals in 2023.

VALERIE CAGLE
Softball

As both a pitcher and a hitter, **CAGLE** is one of the best overall players in her sport. In 2022 and 2023, she was the Atlantic Coast Conference Player of the Year, even as she battled a shoulder injury that needed surgery. In 2023, she was the national player of the year. Cagle also led Team USA to the 2021 U-18 Women's Softball World Cup, where she was the tournament MVP.

NATHAN CHEN
Figure Skating

Chen has been America's biggest men's star in figure skating for almost a decade. He grew up in Salt Lake City, Utah, where he started skating when he was three. He later added ballet training—that's why he is so graceful and flowing on the ice! **CHEN** was a two-time national junior champ before winning a record six US national senior championships in a row. After earning a bronze in the team event at the 2018 Olympics, he soared to gold in the individual skate at the 2022 Olympics.

CAITLIN CLARK Basketball

Long-range shooting and amazing ball handling made **CLARK** the biggest sports story of early 2024. The University of Iowa star led her team to a runner-up finish in the NCAA tournament in 2023. Then in 2024, she became the all-time career scoring leader in her sport—for men or women! Watch for her to take the Women's Basketball Association (WNBA) by storm, too.

GERRIT COLE

Baseball

Since he joined Major League Baseball (MLB) in 2013, **COLE** has been one of baseball's top pitchers. He earned three All-Star selections and an ERA (earned run average) title with the Pittsburgh Pirates and later the Houston Astros. He started his career with Pittsburgh and Houston and helped the Astros win the 2019 AL title. Cole moved to the New York Yankees and led the AL with 16 wins in 2021. Always a hard-throwing fireballer, he earned his second league strikeout total, too. He had his best season in 2023 when he led the AL in innings pitches and ERA and won his first Cy Young Award. He has earned a total of six All-Star selections.

THIBAUT COURTOIS — Soccer

This tall, intelligent player from Belgium is the world's best goalkeeper. Teams that he plays for have won title after title; his shot-stopping skills are a big reason why. **COURTOIS** won Spain's La Liga title with Atlético de Madrid. He won two Premier League championships with Chelsea before returning to Spain to play for Real Madrid. Guess what? He won two *more* titles. In 2022, he won the Yashin Trophy as the top goalie in the sport. For his national team, he has played in three World Cups.

RYAN CROUSER

Track and Field

Fans at a Grand Prix track meet in Los Angeles in 2023 could not believe their eyes. They knew **CROUSER** was one of the best ever at the throwing sport of shot put. He had already won two Olympic gold medals, after all. But at the LA meet, he put on an amazing show. He put the shot six times. Three of the throws were the longest ever, including a new world record of 23.56 meters (77 feet and 3.55 inches)! A shot put weighs sixteen pounds . . . can you imagine throwing that so far?

STEPHEN CURRY — Basketball

This Golden State Warrior has changed what people thought a basketball player can do. No one has made more three-point shots in NBA history, and no one has made as many types of amazing long-range buckets as **CURRY**. He's more than just a shooter, though. Curry's all-around game—passing, dribbling, defense—has helped the Warriors win four NBA titles and earned him nine NBA All-Star selections. Curry grew up around the game; his dad, Dell, played sixteen NBA seasons. (Curry's brother, Seth, is also a solid NBA player.) Curry first lit up the scoreboard at Davidson University, where he set a national college single-season record for three-pointers and led the nation in scoring. By 2012–13, in his fourth season for the NBA, he was the league leader in three-point baskets. He set a single-season record with 402 in 2015–16 and has led the league seven times. He also has the most career threes with more than 3,400 of them. He has led the league in scoring, steals, and free-throw percentage. His trophy case includes two NBA MVP trophies, along with All-Star Game and NBA Finals MVPs. If you're a basket, Steph Curry will find you!

NOVAK DJOKOVIC — Tennis

This powerful right-handed player has won more Grand Slam singles titles than any other player. For almost twenty years, the native of Serbia has dominated men's tennis. After starting to play when he was just four years old, he quickly became a youth star. He turned pro in 2003 and began winning . . . and he has never stopped. **DJOKOVIC'S** first Grand Slam singles title came in the '08 Australian Open, and he has won that tournament nine times since. So far, he has seven Wimbledon titles, four US Opens, and three French Opens. That total of twenty-four singles titles means he's a champ on hardcourts, grass, and clay. No male player has been No. 1 for more than Djokovic's 389 weeks through the end of 2023. And here's a piece of trivia: A newly discovered beetle was named *Duvalius djokovici* in his honor!

LUKA DONČIĆ
Basketball

Few players are as versatile on a basketball court as this native of Slovenia. **DONČIĆ** grew up in a hoops family—his dad was a pro player in Serbia. He was so good so fast that he signed with Spain's Real Madrid club when he was just thirteen, and he was on the senior team at sixteen! When he was nineteen, he was drafted in the first round by the NBA's Dallas Mavericks. He was the 2018–19 NBA Rookie of the Year, and has since earned four straight All-Star selections and four first-team All-NBA nods. Dončić is six feet, seven inches but plays like a small guard, with a grab bag of no-look passes and quick-step drives to the hoop.

KATE DOUGLASS

Swimming

At the Olympics in 2021 in the 200-meter medley, **DOUGLASS** earned a bronze medal—but she has her eyes on more. She is a rare swimmer who can win at almost every stroke. While swimming for the University of Virginia, she was called one of the greatest college swimmers ever, with four individual and four relay national championships.

CAELEB DRESSEL

Swimming

At the 2017 World Aquatics Championships, **DRESSEL** won seven gold medals, including freestyle, butterfly, and medley races. He picked up six more golds at the 2019 Worlds. In all, he has earned fifteen world championship golds. Dressel had big success at the Tokyo Games, which were held in 2021. He was the first Olympic swimmer ever to win the 50 free, 100 free, and 100 butterfly. He won two relay golds to bring his career record to an amazing seven Olympic golds.

25

CRYSTAL DUNN
Soccer

In soccer, the goal scorers get all the headlines. But experts know it's the solid defenders who are the heart of a team. Since 2016, the left back for the US Women's National Team has usually been this New York native. In more than 70 games for the US, **DUNN** has taken part in two Olympic Games and has helped the team win one Women's World Cup and five SheBelieves Cups. She's been a pro since 2014, when she joined the National Women's Soccer League (NWSL). Versatile, dependable, and a real leader, Dunn is US soccer's secret star.

MARIAH DURAN
Skateboarding

When she was ten, **DURAN** got her first skateboard. It changed her life. She began learning tricks and new ways to ride, and was quickly winning competitions. She won her first X Games gold medals in 2018. In 2021, she was on the US team that skated at the Tokyo Olympics. In 2023, she won again at the X Games after coming back from an ankle injury.

KEVIN DURANT
Basketball

This fourteen-time NBA All-Star has been amazing his fans since he was in college with his excellent outside shooting and all-around game. The national player of the year at the University of Texas, **DURANT** became a four-time NBA scoring champ (and the 2014 NBA MVP) with Oklahoma City. He joined the Warriors in 2016 and helped them win two titles, while earning the Finals MVP award both times.

JAGGER EATON
Skateboarding

Talk about an early start! **EATON** was just eleven in 2012 when he became the youngest skater at the X Games at the time. He grew into a skater who is good at all events, winning X Games gold in street (2017) and park (2022). In 2021, Eaton earned a bronze medal at the Tokyo Olympics. Incredibly, he was skating that day with broken bones in his ankle. Ouch!

CHASE ELLIOTT
Auto Racing

Elliott comes from racing royalty. His father, Bill, was a successful and popular NASCAR driver for thirty-eight years. **ELLIOTT** took up the sport as a kid and made it to NASCAR's top series in 2015. He got his first race win in 2018 and had reached eighteen career victories by 2023. His best season came in 2020 when he won the Chase for the Cup Championship race to win the season title, matching his dad's 1988 title. Like his dad, he has been named NASCAR's most popular driver six times.

JOEL EMBIID

Basketball

One of the NBA's top big men since joining the Philadelphia 76ers in 2016, **EMBIID** had a slow start: He was drafted from his native country, Cameroon, in 2014, but a foot injury kept him out for two seasons. When he finally took the court, success came fast! He was an All-Star in his second season and every year since. In 2021–22, he became the first player born outside the US to win the NBA scoring title. He repeated as scoring champ in 2022–23, and also won his first NBA MVP award in 2023.

ERICA ENDERS

Auto Racing

One of only a few women in the superfast drag racing sport, **ENDERS** is one of the overall best drivers. Since she began in 2005, she's been winning checkered flags and titles in the Pro Stock Division. Her car can reach more than 210 mph in only a thousand feet. In 2022, Enders had the fastest race in Pro Stock history at only 6.45 seconds. Talent like that has earned her six national championships through 2023.

JOHN JOHN FLORENCE — Surfing

Born on an island surrounded by waves, **FLORENCE** was riding Hawaii's surf by the age of four. His mom also surfed. Florence loved the sport and started competing with the best. He was only thirteen when he became a pro surfer. In 2016, he was the world champion, and repeated the title in 2017. He does his best work on the biggest waves and most radical pipelines in the world. Florence was on the US team at the Tokyo Olympics, too.

COCO GAUFF

Tennis

In 2023, **GAUFF** reached the top of the tennis world with her exciting victory at the US Open. She was only nineteen, but had been aiming at this goal since she was just a kid. Gauff turned pro when she was fifteen and beat one of her idols, Venus Williams. Later that year, she won her first pro tournament, an indoor event in Austria. She worked her way up the ranks and had her best season yet in 2023. She won three events and capped off the year with her US Open triumph. What's next for this young superstar?

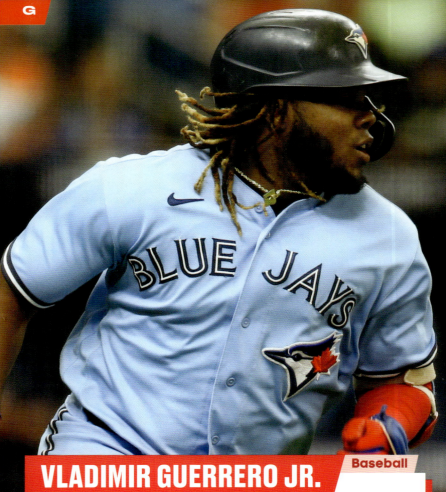

VLADIMIR GUERRERO JR.

Baseball

Following a famous dad can be hard to do. Vladimir Sr. played sixteen great MLB seasons, ending up in the Baseball Hall of Fame. **GUERRERO JR.** is off to a pretty great start, too! A first baseman and DH (designated hitter), he started with the Toronto Blue Jays in 2019. Two years later, he was the AL home-run champ with 48 dingers. He also earned the first of his three All-Star selections. In 2023, he thrilled fans everywhere by blasting 72 taters when he ended up on top at the All-Star Home Run Derby.

ERLING HAALAND

Soccer

Sometimes it takes a big stage to reveal a star. **HAALAND** is from Norway. He began his pro career there before playing in Germany for four seasons. He piled up 27 goals for Dortmund in 2020–21, but it was kind of under the radar. Then, in 2022–23, he joined Manchester City in the English Premier League, and well . . . he went wild. Haaland set a single-season record with 36 goals (in only 35 games!). He had four hat tricks, the most in a season since 1996. He also needed only 25 games to reach 30 Champions League (CL) goals, also a new record. Haaland has twice led the CL in goals, earning the Golden Boot. His six-five size, his incredible speed, and his nose for the goal make him a nightmare for defenses, and a dream come true for City fans.

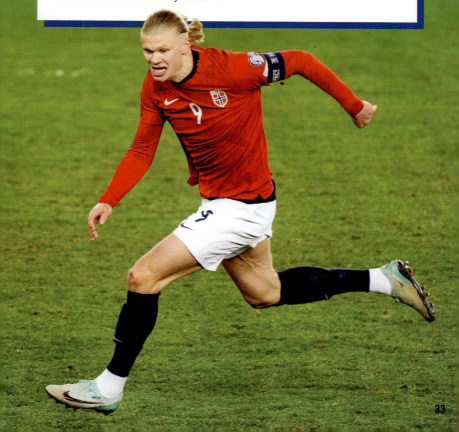

ANNA HALL

Track and Field

The heptathlon is one of the hardest events in sports. In two days, an athlete has to complete seven different track-and-field events. She has to run fast, jump high, and throw things a long way. **HALL** is one of the world's best heptathletes. She was the NCAA champion at the University of Florida and has won silver and bronze at the World Championships. She's also a five-time national indoor and outdoor champ.

JAMES HARDEN
Basketball

The most famous beard in sports can't hide this all-around hoops star's talent. **HARDEN'S** beard is so famous, it even had its own social media account for a while! Harden joined the Oklahoma City Thunder in 2009 out of Arizona State. With Oklahoma, he was the Sixth Man of the Year in 2011–12. Once he moved to the Houston Rockets in 2012, he really shined, winning three NBA scoring titles, while also becoming one of the league's best passers, leading the league in assists per game twice. He's never met a shot he didn't like, whether raining threes or driving to the hoop. By 2018, he was the NBA MVP. He went on to play for the Brooklyn Nets, the Philadelphia 76ers, and the Los Angeles Clippers. This ten-time All-Star remains an all-around hoops threat.

BRYCE HARPER

Baseball

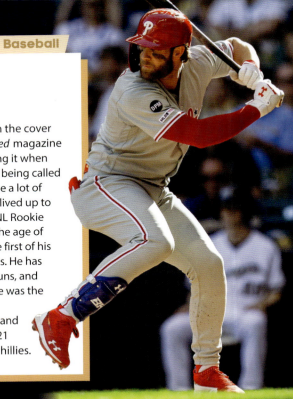

Seeing yourself on the cover of *Sports Illustrated* magazine is an honor. Seeing it when you're only sixteen and being called the "Chosen One" can be a lot of pressure. **HARPER** has lived up to that hype. He was the NL Rookie of the Year in 2012 (at the age of twenty) and earned the first of his seven All-Star selections. He has led the NL in homers, runs, and on-base percentage. He was the 2015 NL MVP with the Washington Nationals, and an NL MVP again in 2021 with the Philadelphia Phillies.

DERRICK HENRY

Football

When **HENRY** has the ball and a head of steam . . . watch out! This man has been a top running back since he became a starter in 2018. He plays a tough position, so his record of leading the NFL in carries three times is impressive. More impressive is his yardage total, where he has been the top for two seasons. In 2020, the Tennessee Titan star rumbled for 2,027 yards, the fifth most of all time. He also led the NFL in touchdowns (TDs) in 2019 and 2020.

LINDSEY HORAN
Soccer

Hard-charging but super skilled, **HORAN** has become one of the top women's players in the world. A midfielder, she joined the US Women's National Team in 2013, and has helped them win the 2019 Women's World Cup, a Confederation Championship, and five SheBelieves Cups. Horan played five seasons in the NWSL, winning a title with the Portland Thorns. Since 2021, she has played with the Lyon team in France, where she has helped them win two league titles and a Champions League trophy.

JALEN HURTS
Football

One of football's most exciting players, **HURTS** really made his mark in 2022, leading the Philadelphia Eagles to the Super Bowl and nearly coming home with the trophy. Hurts took over as the Philly starting quarterback (QB) in 2021, his second season, and has shown off multiple talents. He's an accurate passer who throws very few interceptions. His speed also makes him an elite runner, scoring 26 TDs on the ground in his first three seasons.

NYJAH HUSTON — Skateboarding

Few skaters have been as successful as **HUSTON**. He first made news by reaching the X Games when he was only eleven years old. He's been among the world's best street skaters since, winning a record thirteen X Games gold medals and six World Championships. Along the way, he gained fans in and out of skateboarding, helping the sport rise in popular culture. He was also a pioneer in attracting more Black skaters. Though he was disappointed not to medal at the Tokyo Olympics, Huston remains a good bet to win any event he enters.

SABRINA IONESCU

Basketball

A triple-double is one of the hardest feats to achieve in hoops. In a single game, a player has to reach double digits in three stat categories—usually points, assists, and rebounds. In college at the University of Oregon, **IONESCU** made it look easy. She had 26 triple-double games, setting a new NCAA career record among men and women. After missing her first WNBA season (2020) because of an injury, she has kept up her all-around play with three triple-doubles (so far!) as a pro. She's a two-time All-Star with the New York Liberty, and in 2023, set a new WNBA single-season record with 128 three-pointers.

LAMAR JACKSON — Football

Since he joined the Baltimore Ravens in 2018, **JACKSON** has been a two-way threat. He was a star QB at Louisville in college, but some scouts thought his style of play was not perfect for the NFL. They were wrong! In his second season, Jackson led the NFL in TD passes *and* set an NFL QB record with 1,206 rushing yards. No surprise that he was the NFL MVP that season. He topped 1,000 yards again in 2020, a back-to-back feat no other QB has ever done. Through the air or on the ground, Jackson is an offensive threat.

JUSTIN JEFFERSON

Football

In his short NFL career, **JEFFERSON** has become one of the most exciting players in the sport. He is "only" six feet, one inch tall, but he plays like a giant. He has great leaping ability and can make catches at any angle. Jefferson burst onto the scene with 1,400 receiving yards as a rookie with the Minnesota Vikings in 2020. By 2022, he was the Offensive Player of the Year after leading the NFL with 1,809 receiving yards and 128 catches. When the Vikings come to town, defensive backs know they are in for a tough day.

LEBRON JAMES — Basketball

A few people might disagree, but here's a popular take: LeBron **JAMES** is the best basketball player of all time. In twenty-one seasons, he has become the NBA's all-time leading scorer and is the only player to lead three different teams to NBA titles. James got off to a hot start, winning the Rookie of the Year award in 2004 after jumping right from high school to the Cleveland Cavaliers. He won the first of three All-Star Game MVP trophies in 2006 and was a six-time All-Star and a scoring champ. But he felt like he needed to leave Cleveland to get a ring.

After joining the Miami Heat, James won back-to-back NBA titles and Finals MVP awards in 2012 and 2013. But he had grown up near Cleveland and really wanted to bring a title to his hometown, so he returned to the Cavs in 2014—and won the championship in 2016! Always seeking a new challenge, he jumped to the Los Angeles Lakers in 2018, and helped them win the 2020 NBA title (of course, he was the Finals MVP, again).

A four-time league MVP, too, James took over the all-time scoring crown in 2023. He is as powerful a leader as he is a dominant scorer inside and outside—and he's a fierce defender.

AUTHOR'S NOTE: Sorry, Michael Jordan fans, James is the King of Basketball!

NIKOLA JOKIĆ — Basketball

Players as big as **JOKIĆ** is (six feet, eleven inches and almost three hundred pounds) are not supposed to be as nimble as he is. But in eight NBA seasons, this native of Serbia has changed how big men play. Jokić has dominated at both ends, playing great defense, while also scoring from inside and outside. But it's his passing skills that really make him special. He sees passing lanes that no one else does, and teammates have to be ready for the ball at all times. He earned the first of his six All-Star selections in 2019. Jokić was the NBA MVP in 2021 and 2022, but he got what he really wanted in 2023: He led the Denver Nuggets to their first NBA championship.

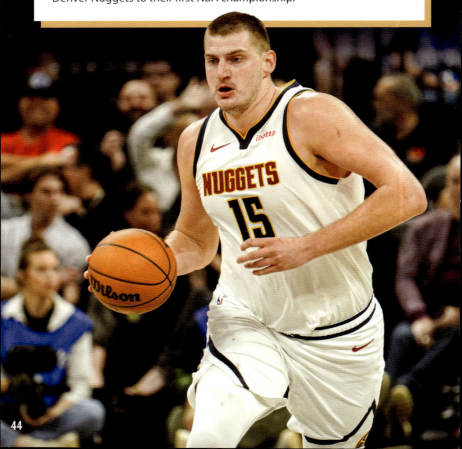

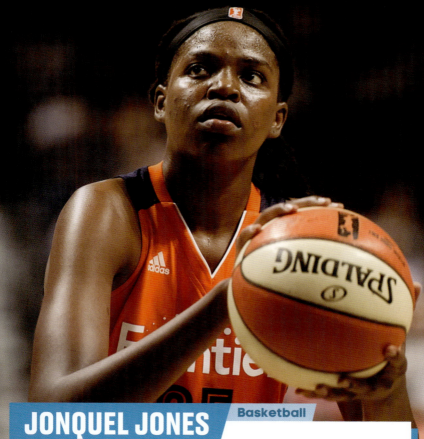

JONQUEL JONES **Basketball**

A steady move upward: That's what **JONES'S** WNBA career has been. A first-round pick by the Connecticut Sun in 2016, she was an All-Star in her second season, when she also won the Most Improved Award. In 2018, Jones was named the league's Sixth Woman, an award given to the top sub in the league. By 2021, she was a regular starter and earned the WNBA MVP trophy, largely for her dominant defense and rebounding skills. Jones helped the Sun reach the WNBA Finals in 2022, but they lost. She moved to the powerhouse New York Liberty in 2023 and made it to another Finals.

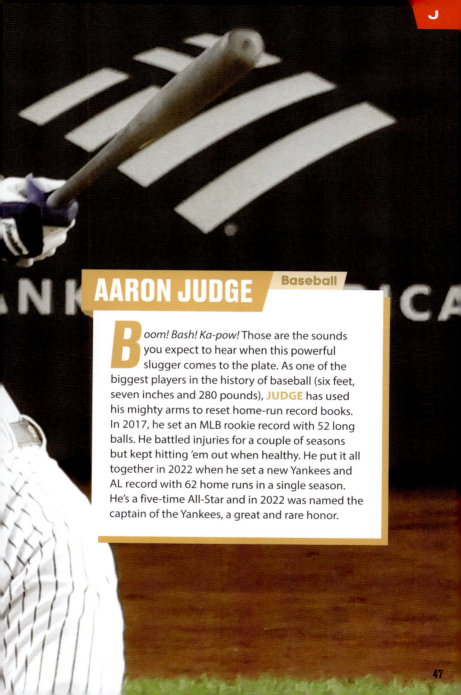

AARON JUDGE — Baseball

Boom! Bash! Ka-pow! Those are the sounds you expect to hear when this powerful slugger comes to the plate. As one of the biggest players in the history of baseball (six feet, seven inches and 280 pounds), **JUDGE** has used his mighty arms to reset home-run record books. In 2017, he set an MLB rookie record with 52 long balls. He battled injuries for a couple of seasons but kept hitting 'em out when healthy. He put it all together in 2022 when he set a new Yankees and AL record with 62 home runs in a single season. He's a five-time All-Star and in 2022 was named the captain of the Yankees, a great and rare honor.

K

TRAVIS KELCE
Football

Combining size, speed, and pass-catching skill, **KELCE** has become one of the top tight ends in NFL history. Kelce has seven straight 1,000-yard seasons, a first for tight ends. He got 1,416 of those yards in 2020 to set the single-season record, too. Kelce had a TD catch in each of the first two Super Bowl wins by the Kansas City Chiefs, and he has been to eight Pro Bowls. Kelce had nine catches when the Chiefs won a third Super Bowl after the 2023 season.

SAM KERR
Soccer

Few players in soccer history have had a nose for the goal like this Australian legend. She was nineteen when she joined the NWSL, where she played for seven seasons. **KERR'S** 77 goals still stand as the record number of all-time goals. Kerr moved to England in 2019 and has led Chelsea to four first place finishes in a row, piling up more than 99 goals through early 2024. In 2022, she became her country's all-time leader in goals; she has led the Matildas to three Women's World Cups, where she scored six.

CHLOE KIM
Snowboarding

When you aim to be one of the best of all time, why wait to get started? **KIM** was only fourteen when she burst onto the snowboarding scene with a SuperPipe gold at the 2015 X Games. She added world championship and Junior Olympic titles, thrilling fans with her high-flying, twisting, creative skills on the half-pipe. In 2018, she won a Winter Olympics gold medal—then she repeated gold in 2022, even though every competitor was aiming to take her down. Kim's success has made her one of the few winter sports stars to earn wide recognition.

HILARY KNIGHT

Ice Hockey

One of the best women's hockey players ever, **KNIGHT** first zoomed to fame by helping the University of Wisconsin win two NCAA national titles. Then she was the first American player to be named MVP in the Canadian Women's Hockey League. When a US league began in 2015, Knight (of course) was its first scoring champ, and her team won the title. With the US national team, Knight has played in four Olympics, winning three silvers and one gold (2018). In 2023, she was the captain of the US team that won its ninth World Championship, and was named the world player of the year.

LYDIA KO — Golf

Born in South Korea, **KO** moved with her family to New Zealand when she was very young. She started playing golf at age five. When she was fourteen, she was the youngest player ever to win a pro event. She joined the Ladies Professional Golf Association (LPGA) in 2014. At eighteen, Ko won the 2015 Evian Championship, one of the five "majors" in women's golf. She was the youngest person to win a major since 1868! She won her first LPGA Player of the Year award that season, too, and another in 2022. Ko has won nineteen LPGA events through 2023 and thirteen more in other international tours.

NELLY KORDA — Golf

A solid young pro golfer, **KORDA** really burst onto the scene in 2021. That year, the American star won her first major (the Women's PGA Championship) and three other LPGA tournaments, and she reached the top of the world golf rankings for the first time. She even won the gold medal at the Tokyo Olympics and played on the US Solheim Cup team. Korda had won her first LPGA tournament in 2018. That matched a win by her sister, Jessica, also an LPGA player.

L

ROSE LAVELLE — Soccer

On a US Women's National Team packed with goal-scoring stars, **LAVELLE** is the glue that holds it all together. Since joining the US team in 2017, she has become its creative playmaker in midfield. Her biggest success came at the 2019 Women's World Cup. She was named the tournament's No. 3 overall player, and her goal in the final clinched the championship for the US over the Netherlands. She also played for the US in the 2023 Women's World Cup and won a bronze medal with the team at the Olympics in 2021.

TREVOR LAWRENCE — Football

Talk about getting off to a hot start: As a college freshman, **LAWRENCE** led Clemson to a national championship. He hasn't slowed down much since. He threw for more than 10,000 yards in three seasons and Clemson reached the College Football Playoffs twice more. Lawrence was the Jacksonville Jaguars' No. 1 overall pick in 2021. He struggled as a rookie, leading the NFL with 17 interceptions, but he bounced back in 2022. Lawrence had 25 TD passes and led the Jags to the playoffs, including a wild-card win over the LA Chargers. He will likely be a top NFL QB for many years.

KATIE LEDECKY
Swimming

You're looking at the greatest swimmer in women's sports history. No woman has won more than **LEDECKY'S** sixteen individual and twenty-one overall world championship gold medals. She's also second all-time among female swimmers with seven Olympic gold medals. At one point, she had the top thirty 800-meter freestyle swim times ever! Ledecky started swimming races when she was only six years old. She was so focused on improving that she left notes around her room with her swimming goals on them. After winning a stack of junior championships, she surprised many experts when she made the 2012 US Olympic team in the 800 meters. Then she shocked the world by beating the defending champ in the event and earning her first gold medal. Success didn't change her, though, and she went back to swim for her high school team. In 2013, Ledecky won the first of her world championship medals. In 2016, she joined Stanford University and helped them win a pair of NCAA championships before she turned pro. Ledecky is a five-time World Swimmer of the Year, among dozens of other honors. She's aiming to add to her amazing record, so look for more gold ahead!

SUNISA LEE

Gymnastics

The best athletes step up when the spotlight hits them, even if it's a surprise. At the Olympics in 2021, the world expected Simone Biles (page 10) to aim for another gold. But she had to pull out for health reasons. Her teammate **LEE** stepped up. Lee had a top score on the uneven bars as the US won a team silver medal. In the all-around final, Lee won the gold! Lee's family is Hmong, and Lee was the first Hmong American to win an Olympic medal. She had been aiming at the Games since winning team gold and floor exercises silver at the 2019 World Championships. After battling back from a foot injury, she was golden in 2021.

JESSICA LONG

Swimming

She's the most dominant Paralympic swimmer in the world. Born in Russia, **LONG** lost the bottom half of her legs to a medical disorder when she was very young, not long after she was adopted by her American parents. She grew up in Maryland and participated in a lot of sports, but was best at swimming. She was only twelve when she won three golds at the 2004 Paralympics. At only fifteen, Long was named the top overall amateur athlete in the US in 2007. Among her sixteen Paralympic golds are wins in freestyle, butterfly, and individual medley. She also has thirty-seven world championship gold medals.

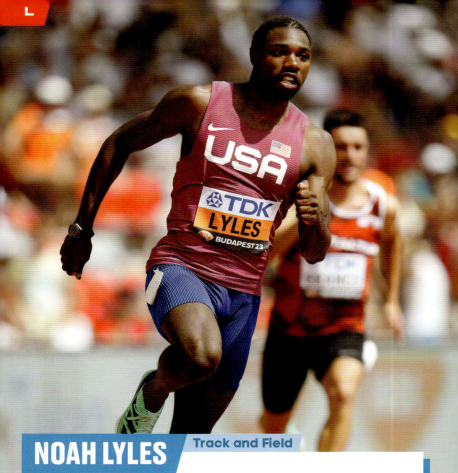

NOAH LYLES — Track and Field

Watch for this talented sprinter to be a breakout star. **LYLES** dazzled at the Olympics in 2021, earning a bronze in the 200 meters. At the 2023 World Championships, he became the first sprinter since the great Usain Bolt in 2015 to win the 100- and 200-meter races plus gold in the 4 x 100-meter relay. Lyles has six world championship golds in all. His time of 19.31 seconds in the 200 is the fastest ever by an American and third-fastest ever! Will he become the fastest man in the world soon?

CATARINA MACARIO

Soccer

In her young career, **MACARIO** has been a star on three continents. She grew up in Brazil, but at the time that country did not offer a lot of support to women athletes. So the teenage soccer star moved with her family to the US. Since 2020, she has been a goal-scoring spark for the US Women's National Team, helping it win two SheBelieves Cups. As a pro in Europe, she helped Lyon win the French league title. An injury made her miss the 2023 Women's World Cup, but she returned to the field in 2024 with Chelsea, in England.

NATHAN MacKINNON

Ice Hockey

The Colorado Avalanche center has been a solid goal scorer since he was the 2014 National Hockey League (NHL) Rookie of the Year. Playing nearly all of Colorado's games, **MacKINNON** has earned seven All-Star Game selections. His best season came in 2021–22 when he led Colorado to a Stanley Cup championship. He had a career-best 111 points in 2022–23. At every Avalanche game, look for MacKinnon around the net!

PATRICK MAHOMES
Football

Electric and creative, **MAHOMES** has been an exciting player since he took over as the Chiefs' starting QB in 2018. That year, he was the NFL MVP. He led the NFL with 50 TD passes and also had 5,097 passing yards. He was already showing off his many unique ways of throwing: sidearm, left-handed, no-look, and more. A six-time Pro Bowl choice, he has led the Chiefs to six straight American Football Conference Championship Games through the 2023 season. They won four and went on to win Super Bowls for the 2019, 2022, and 2023 seasons. The Chiefs were the first back-to-back champs in nineteen seasons. Mahomes is one of the most popular and impressive stars in America's most popular sport.

CALE MAKAR — Ice Hockey

He might be a young player, but **MAKAR** is already one of the best defensemen in hockey. A native of Canada, he won the Calder Trophy as the NHL's top rookie in 2020. Two years later, Makar had a dream season, winning the Norris Trophy as the top defender. Then he led Colorado to a Stanley Cup title and won the Conn Smythe Trophy as the playoff MVP. Watch for this tough, lightning-quick player to grab more trophies in the future.

AUSTON MATTHEWS

Ice Hockey

Though he was born in the United States, **MATTHEWS** plays for the Toronto Maple Leafs in Canada. He was only nineteen when he won the 2017 Calder Trophy as the top rookie, playing every game and scoring 40 goals. In 2020–21, Matthews led the NHL with 41 goals and finished second in the MVP voting. He led again in 2021–22 with a career-best 60 goals and won the Hart Trophy as the MVP. He's a steady, high-scoring force who aims to bring the Cup home to Canada.

KYLIAN MBAPPÉ

Soccer

One of soccer's most exciting players started in the French league when he was sixteen. **MBAPPÉ** made his first big splash at the 2018 World Cup. France won the title as he became the second teenager ever to score in the final game. By the time he scored eight goals at the 2022 World Cup (where France finished second), he was an international superstar. His nose for the goal has also helped Paris-Saint Germain (PSG) win five French league championships—he has three seasons with 25 or more goals! Mbappé uses his great speed and dribbling skills to set up incredible shots.

CONNOR McDAVID

Ice Hockey

Even before he reached the NHL's Edmonton Oilers in 2015, **McDAVID** was set to be a star. He set junior hockey records in Canada everywhere he played. Once he reached the NHL, he lived up to the hype. By his second season, he was the league leader with 100 points and won the first of his three NHL MVP trophies. He's been an All-Star all nine seasons and has led the league in points a total of five times. His 2022–23 total of 153 points is one of the top totals in league history. McDavid is already on the list of hockey's all-time greats.

TATYANA McFADDEN

Track and Field

She has covered thousands of miles in her racing wheelchair, but the most important miles **McFADDEN** has traveled were those from Russia to America. She was born in an orphanage with spina bifida, a spinal condition that meant her legs did not work. When she was six, she was adopted. She quickly found that she loved going fast. Her breakthrough came at the 2012 Paralympics, where she won three gold medals. McFadden's career includes twenty Paralympic medals in wheelchair racing (plus one in cross-country skiing). Her powerful arms have also helped her win multiple marathons.

RORY McILROY

Golf

A native of Northern Ireland, **McILROY** is one of the most successful golfers of the past decade. He won his first Professional Golf Association (PGA) Tour event in 2010 and has added twenty-three since then. He also wins regularly on the European tour. Golfers all aim at the four majors, and McIlroy has won those four, including two PGA Championships, a US Open, and a British Open. McIlroy represented his country at the Olympics in 2021, and played for Europe in seven Ryder Cups.

SYDNEY McLAUGHLIN-LEVRONE

Track and Field

The 400-meter hurdles is a tough event. Not only does an athlete have to sprint a full lap of the track, she has to jump over ten wooden barriers. No woman in history has done that faster than this rising American star. No one had finished the race faster than 52 seconds until **McLAUGHLIN-LEVRONE** did it while winning the gold at the Olympics in 2021 (she also won gold in the 4 x 400-meter relay). Then she topped herself by finishing in a world-record 50.86 seconds to win the 2022 World Championships.

DANIIL MEDVEDEV

Tennis

Tennis has been dominated by Roger Federer, Rafael Nadal, and Novak Djokovic for almost twenty years. In 2022, this Russian star finally broke through to reach the No. 1 ranking. Tall for a tennis player at six feet, six inches, **MEDVEDEV'S** biggest win was the 2021 US Open, one of the Grand Slam events. He has also won nineteen other tournaments using his powerful, high-speed serve to score lots of points.

LIONEL MESSI

Soccer

How lucky we are to be able to watch the greatest soccer player of all time—right here in the USA! **MESSI** arrived at FC Miami in Major League Soccer in 2023 and the whole sports world went nuts. He helped a last-place team win or tie the first 11 games he played—and he led them to a Leagues Cup trophy. It was nothing new for Messi. When he was just thirteen, he moved from his home in Argentina to train and play for FC Barcelona. By the time he was sixteen, he was on the senior team. He helped Barcelona win ten Spanish La Liga championships, as well as four Champions League titles. Along the way, he set a record for most goals in a calendar year (91 in 2012), became Barcelona's and La Liga's all-time top scorer, and won a record eight Ballon d'Or trophies as the best player in the world. With his national team, he played in four World Cups before 2022, each time coming oh-so-close to the top trophy. Then in 2022, Messi finally did it. Argentina beat France in penalty kicks, and Messi held up the trophy he had been chasing for decades. Messi's creativity, his nose for the goal, and his ability to make all his teammates better pushed him to the top of the list of soccer GOATs.

YUL MOLDAUER

Gymnastics

One of the most decorated gymnasts in US history, **MOLDAUER** has strength and flexibility. These traits make him a solid competitor in all the men's events. He was a superstar at the University of Oklahoma, winning seven individual championships and three team titles. Moldauer was the 2017 US all-around champ, and has won the famous American Cup trophy three times. He made his Olympic debut in Tokyo in 2021, where he helped the US team finish fifth.

CARISSA MOORE

Surfing

As a kid, **MOORE** had no trouble finding waves to ride—she lived on Hawaii, home to some of the best surf in the world. Training with her dad, she became a junior champion in her teens. When she turned pro at eighteen, she wasted no time, winning the world championship in her first year. She has repeated that feat four times. A big highlight for her came in 2021. Surfing made its first appearance in the Summer Olympics—and Moore won the first gold medal!

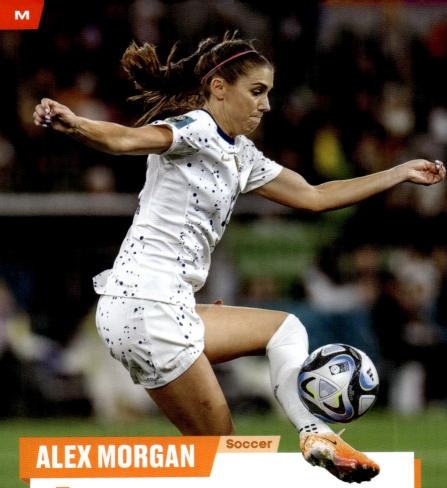

ALEX MORGAN — Soccer

After Abby Wambach retired, **MORGAN** took over as the US national team's main striker. Those are big cleats to fill. All Wambach had done was win a Women's World Cup *and* set a world record for national-team goals. But Morgan has lived up to the challenge. She led the US to victory in the 2015 and 2019 Women's World Cups, and also played in the 2011 and 2023 tournaments. She pounded in six goals and won the Silver Boot in 2019 as the second-best player in the event. Morgan has also played in three Olympics, winning a gold in 2012. Morgan has played eleven seasons in NWSL. She had her best season in 2022, when her 15 goals led the league.

ATHING MU

Track and Field

The 800 meters is one of track's toughest events. Runners have to move at nearly top speed for two whole laps. It takes fast feet and guts to succeed. **MU** has shown that she has both in a very short period of time. In 2021, she won the Olympic gold in the 800 and in the 4 x 400-meter relay. Then she won the 2022 World Championships in the 800. She was only twenty, the youngest person to hold both of those titles.

NEYMAR — Soccer

Like many stars from Brazil, **NEYMAR** goes by one name. As a striker, he had to follow his country's great tradition of high-scoring forwards, such as Pelé, Ronaldo, and Ronaldinho. But in a decade of outstanding play, he has gone even further, becoming Brazil's all-time top goal scorer for the national team. He became a national hero by scoring the gold medal–winning penalty kick in the 2016 Olympics. In his pro career, he starred first for Barcelona, in Spain, helping them win a pair of La Liga titles alongside Lionel Messi. He moved to PSG in 2017 and just kept winning. Joined by Kylian Mbappé, Neymar helped PSG win five more French championships. In 2023, he joined a team in Saudi Arabia.

CHARLOTTE NORTH

Lacrosse

If lacrosse were as widely watched as soccer, **NORTH** would be as famous as Alex Morgan. North was a college superstar, winning two national player-of-the-year awards and helping Boston College win the 2021 national title. Her 358 career goals were the most in US college history, too. An attack (forward position) with incredible stick skills, speed, and strength, look for North to help the US women's national team achieve new heights.

SHOHEI OHTANI — Baseball

Hitting a baseball is very hard to do. Only a very few athletes can master the skill and become All-Stars. Pitching is also difficult; it takes a lot of practice and effort to become a superstar. Usually, players are one or the other. Then there's **OHTANI**. Since he was a high school star in his native Japan, Ohtani has been doing things no players have ever done—excelling as both a pitcher and a hitter. After five seasons in Japan, he was the AL Rookie of the Year with the Los Angeles Angels in 2018. He missed 2019 with an injury, and 2020 was shortened by the COVID-19 pandemic. In 2021, however, he was ready to pitch . . . and hit. He won nine games on the mound with a 3.18 ERA—and hit 46 homers with 100 runs batted in and 26 steals, earning the AL MVP award. Incredibly, he was even better in the next two seasons, finishing second in the MVP voting in 2022 after 15 wins and 34 homers. He won his second MVP trophy in 2023 after an AL-best 44 homers and holding hitters to a .184 batting average. Another arm injury means he'll only be a hitter in 2024 for his new team, the Los Angeles Dodgers. But once he's back on the mound, watch this all-around star keep making history every day.

NAOMI OSAKA — Tennis

Naomi **OSAKA** caught the attention of the world in 2018 when she beat tennis legend Serena Williams in the finals of the US Open to win her first Grand Slam tournament. This power player has aggressive baseline strokes and a huge serve, allowing her to dominate many of her opponents. Osaka has won a total of four Grand Slams, all on hard court. She plays for Japan, which is the country where she was born. When Japan hosted the Olympics in 2021, Osaka became the first tennis player in history to light the Olympic cauldron during an opening ceremony.

MICAH PARSONS

Football

As an NFL rookie in 2021, **PARSONS** burst onto the scene with speed and skills. With 13 sacks, he earned Defensive Rookie of the Year honors. He was even second in the overall Defensive Player of the Year voting, a rare spot for a first-year player. But Parsons is a rare bird. Few players combine his quickness off the ball with "seek-the-QB" football smarts. Every team the Dallas Cowboys play against has to game-plan around his unique talent.

JESSICA PEGULA — Tennis

Most tennis stars peak early in their careers; it's a hard game for "older" players. But **PEGULA** has been a rising star in the game, even as she turned thirty years old in 2024. She's one of the top American players on the women's tour, and regularly makes the late rounds of the top tournaments. In the less-well-known world of doubles tennis, she's an international star, often ranked No. 1 in the world. Sports are in her blood, too; her family owns the NFL's Buffalo Bills.

KELSEY PLUM
Basketball

When she left the University of Washington in 2017, **PLUM** was the all-time NCAA scoring leader. She was the first overall pick of the WNBA draft, but it took her time to adjust to the pro game. In 2022, she put it all together for the Las Vegas Aces. Plum was the All-Star Game MVP, a WNBA First-Team selection, and also led the Aces to the WNBA championship. With the US national team, Plum won two World Cup gold medals. In 2023, she helped the Aces win the WNBA title for the second time.

CRISTIANO RONALDO
Soccer

No one scores goals like **RONALDO**. A native of Portugal, he has become one of the world's greatest soccer players with memorable seasons in England, Spain, and Italy. In his prime, Ronaldo was one of the fastest players in the world, as well as one of the most exciting dribblers. His ability to leap high above defenders also made him a head-ball star. He joined Manchester United in 2003 at the age of only eighteen; by 2007, he led them to the first of three straight league titles and was the Premier League player of the year twice. He also was named world player of the year five times. Moving to Real Madrid in 2009, he kept up his amazing scoring, knocking in 40 or more goals in three separate seasons. He spent four years with Juventus, in Italy, where he won two more titles. Ronaldo now plays with Al-Nassr, in Saudi Arabia. For his national team, Ronaldo is the all-time leading scorer. In fact, his 116 international goals for Portugal are the most ever by a male soccer player. He cemented his status as one of the GOATs by leading Portugal to the 2016 UEFA European Championship. If you're watching Ronaldo, don't blink—you might miss a goal!

JON RAHM — Golf

A native of Spain, **RAHM** has found international success in the United States. He was a two-time college player of the year at Arizona State. He won his first PGA Tour event in 2017 and began a steady climb to the top of the world rankings; he reached No. 1 in 2020. Rahm had his best pro season in 2021, when he led the PGA Tour in money won. He also won his first major tournament at the US Open. He added another major when he came in first at the 2023 Masters.

ARYNA SABALENKA

Tennis

Since reaching the top twenty in 2018, this star has been steadily moving up the tennis rankings. Thanks to her first Grand Slam win at the 2023 Australian Open, **SABALENKA** reached No. 1 that summer for the first time. She was only six years old when she first played after her dad saw a court near their house and suggested they play! She won the Australian Open again in 2024, giving her fourteen Women's Tennis Association (WTA) title wins at the time; she had reached the finals of twelve more.

SCOTTIE SCHEFFLER

Golf

With a powerful, steady swing, **SCHEFFLER** became the No. 1 golfer in the world in 2023. He has finished in the top five of about 30 percent of his pro tournaments. He won six of those events, including the 2022 Masters for his first Grand Slam title. In 2023, he set a record for most money earned in a single year on the PGA Tour, with more than $21 million.

MIKAELA SHIFFRIN

Skiing

In 2023, **SHIFFRIN** became the all-time leader in World Cup skiing wins, reaching a career total of 88. That's more than any skier since the World Cup began in 1966. She also holds the record for top-three finishes, with 138. Shiffrin, who grew up in Colorado, also has six gold medals at the World Championships. After winning one gold each at the 2014 and 2018 Winter Olympics, she struggled at the 2022 Games and came home empty-handed. But she rebounded to win her latest World Cup title in 2023. With five overall Cups, she's tied for the most ever. Shiffrin's best race is the challenging slalom, but she's versatile enough to be the only skier ever to win at least one race in the six different World Cup events.

SOPHIA SMITH
Soccer

She scores . . . and scores . . . and scores! **SMITH** joined the Portland Thorns of the NWSL in 2021. In 2022 and 2023, she was the team's leading scorer and was near the top of the league in goals. The Thorns won the league title in 2022 behind Smith's 14 goals in 18 games and her awesome opening goal in the championship game. She was named the league MVP. Then she was the NWSL goal-scoring champ in 2023. With the US Women's National Team, she is the brightest light in a young crop of talent. At the 2023 Women's World Cup, Smith had two goals in the team's opening-game win.

BREANNA STEWART
Basketball

B-Stew" is one of the most talented players in women's hoops history. First, she was the high school national player of the year. Then, at the University of Connecticut, she dominated—four national titles, four Final Four Most Outstanding Player trophies, three national player of the year awards. As a high-scoring all-around star, **STEWART** was the WNBA 2016 Rookie of the Year. By 2018, she had led the Seattle Storm to the WNBA title and was the league MVP. The Storm won it all again in 2020. Add in a pair of Olympic gold medals with the US team, and you've got a crowded trophy case. Stewart has a great outside shot, but also excellent abilities around the hoop on offense and defense.

SPENCER STRIDER

Baseball

Over and over again, **STRIDER** strikes 'em out! This young Atlanta Braves right-hander has quickly made a mark on the big leagues. In 2022, Strider hit 200 Ks (that's baseball code for strikeouts!) in only 130 innings, the fastest ever. Then he did even better in 2023, taking only 123.3 innings to reach that total. He was also the MLB leader, and made his first All-Star Game. Watch for this hard thrower to be among league leaders for many years.

IGA ŚWIĄTEK

Tennis

With four Grand Slam titles in three years, **ŚWIĄTEK** has emerged as an international star. Her first big win came at the 2020 French Open, when she became the first player from Poland to win a Grand Slam event. She had her best year in 2022, finishing ranked No. 1 in the world after eight tournament wins including two Grand Slams. At the end of 2023, she won the WTA Finals tournament, beating Jessica Pegula in the finals.

DIANA TAURASI

Basketball

Meet the clear choice for the Queen of the Court. In nineteen WNBA seasons, **TAURASI** has put herself atop the record books for most points, free throws, field goals, and three-point baskets. Her WNBA trophies include the 2004 Rookie of the Year, two Finals MVPs, and the 2009 league MVP. A ten-time All-Star, she has led the Phoenix Mercury to three WNBA championships, the second most of all time. Her winning doesn't stop at the WNBA, though. Taurasi is one of the most successful players ever in international games. She has led the US team to five gold medals at the Olympics, along with three world championship titles. Add in a trio of NCAA titles with the University of Connecticut, and you've got one of the GOATs of the game.

JAYSON TATUM
Basketball

After two mostly quiet seasons at the start of his career with the Boston Celtics, **TATUM** has emerged as one of the NBA's best all-around players. He was First Team All-NBA in 2022 and 2023 and has raised his scoring average each season from 2020–21 to 2022–23. A four-time All-Star, he's an offensive force inside and outside, and his defense continues to improve, too. He led the Celtics to the NBA Finals in 2022, but they lost to the Golden State Warriors.

ALYSSA THOMAS
Basketball

Giving is good, right? Well, that makes **THOMAS** a really, really good person. She gave out a WNBA-record 316 assists in 2023. A four-time All-Star, Thomas excels at both ends—she has made five league All-Defensive teams, too. She played college ball at the University of Maryland and has been a star with the Connecticut Sun since joining the team in 2014.

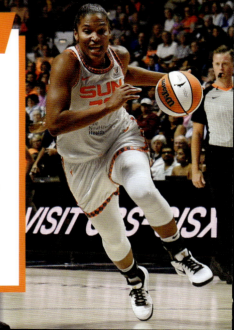

LYLE THOMPSON **Lacrosse**

The sport of lacrosse grew out of an Indigenous American game that has been played in North America for hundreds of years. It has become one of the USA's fastest-growing sports. Young players can look to **THOMPSON** for an example of how it's played. He grew up playing in his Haudenosaunee (a group of six Native American nations) community in New York. At the University of Albany, he was a two-time national player of the year and set an all-time college record with 400 goals. As a pro, he is a three-time Premier Lacrosse League All-Star, as well as a league MVP and team champion. He also stars in indoor lacrosse, earning MVP honors there, too. Playing for the Iroquois National team, he has taken part in three World Championships.

MIKE TROUT — Baseball

Though injuries have slowed him down in recent seasons, **TROUT** continues to be thought of as one of the top overall players in baseball. From 2012 through 2019, he finished first or second in the AL MVP voting seven of eight seasons, winning three times. He's been an All-Star eleven times. Trout is a fantastic all-around hitter, with three AL slugging percentage titles; he can run, leading the AL with 49 steals in 2012 (plus two other 30-steal seasons), and is an outstanding defender. He has played his entire career with the Los Angeles Angels, but even with him, they have made the playoffs only once since he joined them in 2011. Trout was also the 2012 AL Rookie of the Year. Baseball has a stat called WAR, which means "wins above replacement." It measures how much a player contributes to his team over an average player. Trout is third all-time in WAR over a 162-game season.

JUSTIN VERLANDER
Baseball

This hard-throwing right-hander's next stop will be the Baseball Hall of Fame in Cooperstown, New York. In eighteen MLB seasons, he has shown he's a top all-around starter. **VERLANDER** has led the AL in wins, ERA, and strikeouts. He has three Cy Young Awards as the AL's top pitcher, and added the AL MVP in 2011 with the Detroit Tigers. He earned World Series rings in 2017 and 2022 with the Houston Astros, and has been on nine All-Star teams.

MAX VERSTAPPEN
Auto Racing

As Formula 1 has boomed in popularity in the US, **VERSTAPPEN** has become the most famous driver in the sport. He won his first title in the international auto racing series in 2021. It was one of the most exciting finishes in the long history of the sport, as the Dutch driver overtook seven-time champ Lewis Hamilton on the last lap of the last race to win his first title. He repeated in 2022, and then dominated in 2023. That season, he set a record with ten consecutive race wins among his nineteen total wins, which was a single-season record. He clinched the 2023 title with five races left.

LILIA VU
Golf

This American golfer burst onto the pro scene in 2023 with wins in two of the five women's major tournaments. **VU** won the Chevron Championship in a playoff. Then she won the AIG Women's Open by an impressive six shots. The former UCLA star has moved up the ranks quickly, winning three events on the lower-ranked Epson Tour before joining the LPGA in 2019. Another 2023 highlight was helping the US win the international Solheim Cup. Look for more top finishes from Vu.

A'JA WILSON — Basketball

Being "the next big thing" can be a lot of pressure for an athlete. After leading the University of South Carolina to its first NCAA title in 2017, **WILSON** was tagged as a future WNBA star. She was the Las Vegas Aces' first overall draft pick in 2018 . . . and she won the Rookie of the Year award! Wilson dominates at both ends, fighting through for layups and rejecting opponents' shots. She's a five-time All-Star and two-time Defensive Player of the Year. Her all-around play is a big reason the Aces won the 2022 WNBA title. In 2023, Vegas set a league record with 34 regular-season wins. Wilson was then named WNBA Finals MVP when she led her team to another league title.

RESOURCES

Built on the long legacy of TIME, TIME for Kids has been a trusted news source in schools for over 25 years, providing educators with valuable resources for the classroom. From articles about new scientific breakthroughs to profiles on inspiring kids who are helping their communities, TIME for Kids has content to inspire every reader.

For more stories about amazing athletes like the ones you learned about in this book, visit **www.timeforkids.com** and explore the **Sports** section.

INDEX

AUTO RACING
28, 29, 92

BASEBALL
6, 8, 9, 17, 32, 36, 47, 74, 85, 91, 92

BASKETBALL
8, 12, 14, 16, 20, 24, 27, 29, 35, 39, 42, 44, 45, 77, 84, 86, 88, 94

FIGURE SKATING
15

FOOTBALL
7, 13, 36, 37, 40, 41, 48, 53, 60, 76

GOLF
51, 64, 80, 81, 93

GYMNASTICS
11, 56, 68

ICE HOCKEY
50, 59, 61, 62, 63

LACROSSE
73, 89

SKATEBOARDING
26, 28, 38

SKIING
82

SNOWBOARDING
49

SOCCER
12, 18, 26, 33, 37, 48, 52, 59, 62, 67, 70, 72, 78, 84

SOFTBALL
7, 15

SURFING
30, 69

SWIMMING
25, 54, 57

TENNIS
6, 22, 31, 65, 75, 77, 81, 85

TRACK AND FIELD
19, 34, 58, 64, 65, 71